Food For Thought

Morne Campher

Published by Morne Campher, 2022.

While every precaution has been taken in the preparation of this book, the publisher assumes no responsibility for errors or omissions, or for damages resulting from the use of the information contained herein.

FOOD FOR THOUGHT

First edition. October 6, 2022.

ISBN: 979-8215353479

Written by Morne Campher.

Also by Morne Campher

Wisdom For Everyday
The Spirit Filled Life
Food For Thought

Table of Contents

Thanksgiving

I have to thank my heavenly Father. He gave me the idea for this devotional, He gave me the ability to write and He sent people with various skills and the know-how my way. He opened the doors for me. He made a way where there seemed to be no way.

I also want to thank my pastor, Wimpie Helmand. Whenever I had any theological questions, he was ready to answer them. Philip Smith gave me teaching to write about. He also encouraged me to have this book published. Karen Loots organised for these devotionals to be broadcast on community radio stations and she also planned for these devotionals to be recorded.

"This is a plain indication of God's righteous judgment so that you will be considered worthy of the kingdom of God, for which indeed you are suffering."

2 Thessalonians 1: 5

Good News

"For by grace you have been saved through faith, and that not of yourselves, it is the gift of God."

Ephesians 2: 8

Have you ever wondered if you will be going to heaven? Why would you be allowed to enter the pearly gates?

A good number of years ago, I worked with a friend one evening. His grandmother had passed away the previous week. We talked about that and I told him that I wasn't afraid of dying, but that I was afraid of what would happen afterwards. In my mind, it was unfair that some people got to go to heaven while the rest had to suffer for all eternity. Today, I am 100% sure that I'll go to heaven. The good news is that you can be sure as well.

God gave the human race the gift of eternal life. If a friend gives you a gift. You have to accept and take it before it is yours. That begs the obvious question: "How do I accept God's gift of eternal life?"

Before we answer that question, lets look at what the bible says about sin. According to the bible, sin is not only limited to doing something wrong, but it is also saying and thinking the wrong things. Furthermore, the bible also says that one sin is enough to disqualify anyone from going to heaven. Have you ever made an omelet? For argument's sake, lets say you use three eggs in your omelet. Having added the first two eggs to your spice mixture, everything seems to be fine. That is until you break the third egg. It is rotten. No matter how much you try to get rid of it, your whole mixture is spoiled. Lets say I am a super 'holy' man – I only sin three times a day. I drive in the city and somebody cuts me off. I get angry, think that guy is an idiot, show him the finger and curse him. Right there, in that one instance, I fulfilled my daily 'quota.' There are 365 days in a year so that means my sins in one year are 1 095. Lets round it off and say it is 1 000 sins for the year. Now lets say I live to the ripe old age of 80. That is 80 000 sins over my lifetime – and I am a super 'holy' person. One sin disqualifies me, let alone 80 000! That one sin is like the rotten egg that spoiled the whole mixture.

The bible also teaches us that God is righteous, that He can not stand sin. However, the bible also says God is love and that He does not want anybody to be lost; He wants us to go to heaven. That seems absurd. It seems like a contradiction. It is totally impossible for anybody to be without sin. What to do now?

During the middle ages there was a general in Spain that fought against the dictatorship in his country. He traveled, with his army and their families, from village to village. Their food was very limited, so everybody was rationed. One day, one of his lieutenants came to him and said "Sir, we have a problem. Someone is stealing the food." The general didn't have to think about it. He immediately gave the order to his lieutenant to catch whoever is responsible and to punish them. It could not be allowed. After two weeks, the lieutenant returned and said "Sir, I have good news and bad news. The good news is that we caught the person who stole the food. The bad news is that it is your mother." The general knew his mother would not survive the punishment, but neither could he look the other way. Back then, people were tied a pole and received a number of lashes on their backs as punishment. He then said "I'll take my mother's punishment, but let her go." His mother was spared the punishment, but the deed was still punished.

That is exactly how God dealt with sin. In Jesus, sin was punished and we were set free. This is how we accept God's gift of eternal life. We must accept Jesus as our Lord and Saviour. We must trust that He is the only One who will get us there. He is the Way, the Truth and the Life.

If you want to accept God's gift of eternal life, if you want to accept Jesus as your Lord and Saviour, repeat this following prayer. Say it out aloud.

Lord Jesus, I believe that You are the Son of God. Please forgive me all of my sins and come into my heart. In Your Name I pray, Lord Jesus. Amen.

If you said this prayer, you are now saved. Welcome to the family of God. You can now be 100% assured that you will be going to heaven. Just like a new born baby needs to be looked after and grow, so you need to grow in your new-found faith. Find a church that preaches about Jesus and the

Holy Spirit. Read the bible. Spend time with God in prayer. Praise and worship Him. Find other believers and fellowship with them.

Father, thank you for our new brothers and sisters. Please guide them and lead them to where they need to be. May they grow in the knowledge of Your grace. In Jesus' Name I pray. Amen.

Love That Is Deeper Than The Ocean Of The Universe

"For God so loved the world that He gave His only begotten Son, that whoever believes in Him should not perish but have everlasting life."

John 3: 16 (NKJV)

This is a very well-known verse. For me this is pretty vague and not tangible enough. Personal story to put it into perspective.

Years ago I did missionary training. One of my friends came to me and asked if I wanted to go and pray with him. I was under the impression that we'd pray together, so I went.

He then said that we should go our separate ways. I didn't have anything particular on my heart and, to be honest, I didn't want to pray either.

At the time, I really struggled to hear the voice of God. I laid on my back, looked at the stars and said to God "Lord, I am going to lie here until You talk to me." After only a few seconds He started speaking to me. I "heard" His voice inside my mind while at the same I also felt the words in my heart. He said "Imagine you are at the bottom of an ocean. As far as you can see there is only water. How deep do you think this ocean is?" I became very excited, thinking that God was going to tell me the measurements of the universe. He then said "My love for you is deeper than this ocean."

To put a number on it. On YouTube there is a video called 'The Universe Is Bigger Than You Think.' It says the known universe is 93 Billion light years across. A light year is the distance that light travels in a year. A round trip around the earth is about 40 000km. Light travels that distance 7,5 times in one second. Imagine the distance it travels in a year!

In Acts 10: 34 the bible tells us that God does not not favour one person above another or show partiality. This means that God's love for any other person is deeper than the ocean of the universe.

Father thank you for loving me unconditionally. Thank you for having loved me first. Help me Holy Spirit to always meditate on this, especially when times are hard. In Jesus' Name I pray. Amen.

God's Perfect Love

"But God demonstrates His own love toward us, in that while we were still sinners, Christ died for us. Much more then, having now been justified by His blood, we shall be saved from wrath through Him."

Romans 5: 8-9 (NKJV)

God loves people perfectly, all their imperfections, all their flaws and all their failings. It has all been paid for on the cross. God forgave the human race. Some human relationships may be based on the notion that flaws determine the level of love being received. God is not like that. Human flaws, ugliness and sin are mere occasions for God to demonstrate His grace.

People that have accepted Jesus as their Lord and Saviour have been forgiven of their sins. They have been washed clean through the Blood of Jesus. There is no need for people to be embarrassed about their flaws, mistakes and weaknesses. God knows their weaknesses better than they do.

Jesus was tempted in every way, yet He did not sin (Hebrews 4: 15). That means that Jesus can sympathize with all our weaknesses. He does not wait for people to live up to a certain set of dos and dont's in order to love and forgive them. In Romans 5: 8-9 the Bible says that while people were still sinners Jesus died for them. It says that that is proof of God's love.

A butterfly can not morph back into caterpillar. The Blood of Christ has made Christians righteous. They are righteous forever. Falling back into sin does not make a Christian a sinner. Christians are the righteousness of God in Christ. Once the Blood of Jesus has made somebody righteous, that person can not become a sinner again.

All this is proof of God's perfect love.

Lord Jesus, thank you for Your perfect love. You have redeemed me and put me in a right standing with God. In Your Name I pray, Lord Jesus. Amen.

Social Interaction: God's Design

"But Moses' hands became heavy; so they took a stone and put it under him and he sat on it. And Aaron and Hur supported his hands, one on one side, and the other on the other side; and his hands were steady until the going down of the sun."

Exodus 17: 12 (NKJV)

Israel fought a battle in the desert. As long as Moses held his arms up, the Israelites prevailed against their enemy. However, Moses became tired. When he let his arms down, the Israelites started losing. Aaron and Hur saw what was happening. Moses needed help. They could assist him.

Often times people will say something like "You have to do things yourself" or "I don't need anybody's help." However, the bible tells us that we need to look out for each other. We very often need help ourselves. There has certainly been a number of occasions where I needed help.

One morning I wanted to go for a workout at my gym. I got into my car, but the car did not want to start. This was not a problem; it had happened before. The previous time, I sat in the car while my leg was outside. Using that leg, I then pushed the car out of the garage. The driveway was on a slope. As soon as the car hit the downhill, I would bring that leg into the car, close the door, release the clutch and the car would start.

This particular morning I decided to do the same. Again I sat in the car and pushed it. All of a sudden I heard a loud bang. The door had caught in the corner, between the wall and the garage door. It was the only thing that held the car in its position. This was the first opportunity for me to go and get some help. I didn't. Instead, I got out, went to the back of the car, stood with my back against the car and tried to push it all the way back into the garage. However, the floor of the garage was slightly higher than the driveway. I managed to push the car a little bit but just could not get it over the hump.

Realising that I needed some momentum to get it over the hump, I decided to let the car come out further and then push it back. This process I did a few times to no avail. Every time the car would get stuck on the hump. It just did not want to go over. By now the door had swung closed. I was the only thing holding the car back. There was nowhere for me to go.

I realized that I would not be able to hold the car for too long, so I decided to let the car come out completely onto the driveway. My intention was to let it come down the slope while I braked it until the car was in the street. However, the car was much heavier than I and it had built up momentum. It was now pushing me. The car also had a tow bar. As soon as we hit the street I lost my footing and fell. The car went over me into the street. The tow-bar hit my back and the back of my head as I went down. I do not recall that pain. It really happened very fast. I recall losing my footing and then being on the other side of the street with the car above me.

My leg was bent backward as far as it could go. My one foot was stuck somewhere on the underside of the car. I remember feeling this incredible pain in my knee and realizing that my foot was stuck. I knew I had to move forward a bit so that there would be more leeway for my knee and I could then free my foot. As I pulled myself forward the car also moved forward. I was truly stuck. I needed someone to come and push the car off of me. It was a dangerous situation to be in. Another car could have come around the corner, smashed into me and caused even more damage and injury. Fortunately, someone came and pushed the car off of me; I could then unhook my foot.

When I got up my, I saw that my jeans were torn and there was a lot of blood. My glasses was still on my face though. That was a miracle. As I got up I felt a great pain in my foot. However, because of the adrenaline pumping, I was able to walk, only just. Shock also started to set in and I could not think straight. I needed somebody to give me advice, to tell me what I should do next. I then needed somebody to take me to the doctor. X-rays were taken and as it turned out, I had torn all the ligaments in my foot.

Had I gone for help in the first place, all of this could and would have been avoided. I did not and faced the consequences of my decision. Even then, I needed help: somebody to push the car off of me, somebody to help me think straight and somebody to take me to the doctor.

Lord, thank you for Your Spirit. Holy Spirit, thank you for being my Helper. In Jesus' Name I pray. Amen.

Seek God And Live

"For thus says the Lord to the house of Israel: 'Seek Me and live;'"

Amos 5: 4 (NKJV)

Amos was a prophet who saw the sins of Israel. He warned them of God's coming judgment and consequent punishment. The Israelites had turned to the worship of false gods. Even though God had sent many prophets before, the people still did not want to listen.

It is quite significant that Amos mentions three specific places: Bethel, Gilgal and Beersheba. These three places were important sacred cities. They were connected to Israel's walk with God. Bethel was the place where God met with Jacob, Gilgal was the place where God had removed Israel's spiritual reproach during the days of Joshua, and Beersheba was connected to Abraham, Isaac and Jacob. However, these three places had become the epicentre of Israel's worship of false gods. In the same way, we can get so busy with the things of God that we neglect God Himself.

The prophet pleaded with the people to repent and to seek God. This was the only way for the people to be free of God's punishment. It also shows God's willingness to forgive. Once they have done that, there is the promise that they will live. This is true for us today as well. We need to seek God. We need to repent from our sins. It is only in God that we can find life. It is only in Him that we can live.

To seek God means to seek good, to seek righteousness, to seek justice, to worship God and to seek and act upon the Word of God. God will then cause us to live. To live means to enjoy God's mercy, to be free from sinful ways, to have the abundance of life which He has promised and, finally, to have eternal life in heaven.

In the beginning of 2022, a certain ministry held their annual conference. For a whole week the attendees sought God. They worshiped God. As a result, they experienced life. The darkness got pushed out by the light of Jesus. Some received healing in their bodies, some received their sight, some got set free from suicidal thoughts and depression, some received inner healing, people were able to forgive those who hurt them and many financial breakthroughs were also experienced.

Lord, I ask You to help me to always seek You. I want to worship You Lord. I want to offer You worship that is pleasing to You. Help me to seek justice, to behave justly, to seek Your righteousness and be good to others. In Jesus Name, I pray. Amen.

Being Adopted Into God's Family

"And Bethuel begot Rebekah. These eight Milcah bore to Nahor, Abraham's brother."

Genesis 22: 23

Just another boring genealogy, or something more?

Chapter 22 tells the story of God asking Abraham to sacrifice Isaac. So why does the story end with a genealogy?

All Scripture are inspired by the Holy Spirit (2 Timothy 3: 16). In other words, there is a reason why God put that genealogy in there. What is the significance? Abram (God later changed his name to Abraham) was called to leave his home town and go to Canaan. There God made, him a promise. Isaac was the son of that promise.

God now asked Abraham to sacrifice Isaac. Of course, God never required the sacrifice of Isaac, but He tested Abraham's faith and obedience. Abraham passed with flying colours. In this genealogy, Rebekah is mentioned. She became Isaac's wife later on. Instead of Isaac marrying one of the local girls, Abraham sent his servant to his own extended family to find a wife for Isaac. (Another point can be made here about marrying in the family of God, marrying somebody of the same faith). Isaac and Rebekah had a son named Jacob. Jacob's name was later changed to Israel. His sons became the 12 tribes of Israel. Hundreds of years later Jesus was born of the Israelite nation, from the tribe of Judah.

Through faith in Jesus, we become part of God's family. Jesus put us in a right standing with God. As the bible says, we are a "holy nation, a royal priesthood." (1 Peter 2: 9).

"My adopted father still, to this day, recalls the overwhelming emotion he had the moment he held me in his arms and saw my tiny, pink face. They (parents) gave me the best life any child could ever ask for. But more importantly, they gave me unconditional love, a love that was so strong and so natural." This is the true story of someone who was adopted.

Lord Jesus, thank you that You put me in a right standing with God. You made it possible for me to be part of God's family, to be a child of God. In Your Name I pray, Lord Jesus. Amen.

An Attack From Within

"There were also those who said, 'We have borrowed money for the king's tax on our lands and vineyards."

Nehemiah 5: 4 (NKJV)

Nehemiah was called to rebuild the walls of Jerusalem. He was given the resources to do this. It was not plain sailing, however. He faced opposition from Tobiah, Sanballat, the Arabs, the Ammonites and the Ashdodites. However, chapter four ends with a victory for the people. They did the construction with a sword in the one hand.

The devil did not give up. We can see the progression of his strategy – something he still does today. He shifted the attack from the external threats to the internal opposition. When the devil fails in his plans to defeat us externally, he focuses the attack to internal problems and issues.

There was a famine in the land. In spite of the cost of life rising, people still had to pay their taxes. Note, the people did not complain about having to pay taxes. A group of people, some priests among them, took advantage of this. They charged the people exuberant tax amounts. The people had to take out loans in order to afford to live. A number of them defaulted on their loans. It got so bad that people had to sell their sons and daughters into slavery just to make ends meet.

The people started fighting with one another. There was no longer any unity among them. As a result, the work also stopped. Strife had taken a hold of the people. Those charging the interest were greedy.

Nehemiah became aware of these issues and became angry. He was angry because it was not right to charge the exuberant interest rates. He was angry because it led to a lack of unity among the people. He was angry because it stopped God's work.

His response shows a principle of leadership. He became angry, but did not act in anger. He confronted the problem head-on. Nehemiah confronted those who were in the wrong. Nehemiah charged those in the wrong to not only stop the wrongs, but also to restore – to set right the wrongs that were done.

To their credit, the wrong-doers received Nehemiah's rebuke, admitted they were wrong and did the right thing. Words were not enough; it had to be followed by their actions. Each man had to take an oath. These oaths were public. It ensured accountability.

We need to have the same attitude and have a teachable spirit.

Father, I ask that I may be a faithful servant to You. Help me, Holy Spirit, to trust Your Word. Help me to finish the work that You called me to do, to be accountable and to strive for unity. I ask that You would give me a teachable spirit. In the Name of Jesus I pray. Amen.

An Exhortation: Show Mercy To Those Who Doubt

"And on some have compassion, making a distinction;"

Jude 1: 22 (NKJV)

Jude encourages strong believers to exercise and have some sort of judgment. They need to distinguish between those who sincerely doubt and those are just plain rebellious and arrogant.

It should also be noted that Jude warns against false teachers. Even today it is true. There are still false teachers and teachings around. They all proclaim their message under the banner of "Christianity." These teachings sow discord among brethren and turn some away from the truth. The way to effectively "fight" against this is to watch over our own hearts, to remain in God's love.

In his letter, Jude acknowledges that there will be those who doubt. He encourages the believers to show mercy to those who sincerely doubt. Criticism will only drive the doubters further away. It may be that some doubters are on the verge of accepting Jesus as their Lord and Saviour, but still have some lingering questions – questions Christians can answer. As believers, we will do well to remember that it is through mercy that God dealt with our us. We are forgiven, all our sins, we have been set free because of Jesus. God was merciful to us.

Mercy has many characteristics and aspects. Three of the most outstanding characteristics are compassion, patience and concern. However, mercy also includes correction and rebuke. As Christians, we can not ignore sin, but we can be gentle and meek in our approach to the erring brother or sister. Believers should protect each other from the dangers and deceitfulness of sin.

A woman experienced trauma in her life. She had tried various treatments. These treatments only left her with more questions. Eventually, she went for counseling, Christian counseling. The counselors listened to her, helped her and taught her that Jesus loves every part of her. Today, she is a counselor herself, helping others. She testified that "Because I am able to see my heart more clearly, I am able to see God in a much clearer way as well."

Holy Spirit, I pray that I may be able to discern between those who sincerely doubt and those who are rebellious. Help me to be patient with the doubters, to show them mercy. In Jesus Name, I pray. Amen.

Caring For The New-Born

"But we were gentle among you, just as a nursing mother cherishes her own children. So, affectionately longing for you, we were well pleased to impart to you not only the gospel of God, but also our lives, because you had become dear to us."

1 Thessalonians 2: 7-8 (NKJV)

Paul wrote to the congregation in Thessalonica. They were new-born Christians; they had just accepted the Lord Jesus as their Lord and Saviour. He compares the care he and his fellow missionaries gave them to that of a mother caring for and nursing her own children. They fed the Thessalonians wholesome spiritual food. This spiritual food enabled the Thessalonians to develop and grow in Christ.

This responsibility became personal for Paul. Paul did not give the responsibility over to others, he did not get "baby-sitters." He did not substitute his responsibility with books or anything like that, but used his own time and energy to care for them – he made personal sacrifices.

A new Christian can be compared to a new-born baby. That baby can not fend for himself. He needs care. Every new Christian needs nourishment to develop and grow. Discipleship programmes play a big role in this, but the new Christian also needs personal attention and care.

A nursing mother eats food. That food then gets transformed into milk for the baby. In the same way it is important for the care-giver to take in the right kind of spiritual food, the Word of God.

A baseball pitcher played for the Kansas City Royals. It was a farm league, but this pitcher soon got called up to the majors, the big league.

At 22, it was a case of too much too soon. Injuries and a losing season conspired together to him wanting to quit. It also brought back a familiar emotion.

He was the son of a military man. As such, they moved around quite a bit. That led to a lot of build up anger in the young man. In one high school, the anger led to his basketball playing time being cut. It was at this point that he became serious about his relationship with Jesus.

This transformation, along with encouragement from his wife, helped him to push through and not give up. During the mid-season he got traded to Colorado. While in Colorado, he met up with an old friend and started an organization to feed the hungry. That represented a fresh start for him. During his time at Colorado, he went to the world series. It was also the first time that Colorado was in the world series. In 2009, he went to San Francisco. Since then, he was part of three world series championship teams. He still reaches out, feeding the hungry, clothing the poor and providing shelter for the homeless. That pitcher is Jeremey Affeldt.

The people we nurture can become influencers.

Lord, thank you for the gospel that has been preached to me. Thank you that You did not leave me to find my own way, but cared for and nourished me. Lord I pray that I may also be able to care for and provide nourishment to new Christians. In Jesus Name I pray. Amen.

Deadly Consequences

"Behold, I will make you small among the nations; you shall be greatly despised."

Obadiah 1:2 (NKJV)

The prophecy of Obadiah warns against pride, reminds us to place ourselves under God's authority, and implores us to consider the impact of our actions on others. It exhorts us to find hope in being part of God's people. We need to help others in need. God will restore us.

Edom was a strategic country. The high mountains, cliffs, and rocky terrain made it easy to defend. The nation was also a trading hub as it was located on a major travel route. Furthermore, the land was also rich in minerals and natural resources. This combination led to Edom's strength and pride.

Esau was the father of the Edomites. He was the brother of Jacob. Out of Jacob came the Israelites. Despite being brothers, there was a long and bitter dispute between the Israelites and Edomites. They sinned against God and the Israelites, refusing the Israelites passage through their land on their way to the promised land and even helping Israel's enemies against her.

Obadiah means 'Servant of Yahweh.' He prophesied against Edom, warning them of the deceitfulness of their pride: God was going to destroy them. One of Edom's allies turned against her. The attack was humiliating and left them a much smaller nation, both geographically and population-wise. The survivors fled to southern Judea. They were not well treated by the Jews. In AD 70, they were wiped out by the Romans. The prophecy became true.

There was once a scholar who had mastered several languages, studied various ancient scripts, and remembered epic works. A day came when he needed to cross the river. He paid a boatman to take him across. Looking down at the lowly profession of the boatman, the scholar wanted to show his superiority. He asked the boatman if he had ever studied any of the ancient scripts or read an epic work. The boatman replied that he could not read or write and that he did not have the time either. Wanting to show off even more, the scholar then asked if the boatman had at least learned another language. The boatman answered and said that he never left his village and never had the opportunity to learn another language. The scholar remarked with disdain that the boatman had wasted his life by not studying. After some time, the boatman noticed water coming into the boat. He asked the scholar if he had ever learned how to swim. With an arrogant tone, the scholar replied that he did not need that. He could always pay someone to take him across the river. The boatman answered and told the scholar that he had wasted his life, the boat was going to sink, and that he only had enough strength to swim and get himself to the riverbank.

Lord, I thank You for Your Word. Thank you for warning me against pride, arrogance, bitterness and unforgiveness. I ask, Holy Spirit, that You will help me to have a humble heart, love and mercy. In Your Name I pray Lord Jesus. Amen.

God Is Sovereign And A Parent

"Should He repay it according to your terms, just because you disavow it? You must choose, not I; therefore speak what you know."

Job 34:33 (NKJV)

Everybody knows the story of Job. How he was tested and lost everything. Everybody forsook him. Even his friends argued and reasoned with him.

One such friend was Elihu. Elihu challenged Job. Job did not respond to the challenge. To emphasise his point, Elihu repeated the words of Job to the onlookers. In Elihu's mind, the crowd of onlookers would judge Job, based on his own words, and find him guilty. According to him, Job made some rash statements about God's injustice, proving his (Job's) wickedness. Job deserved to be in the situation he was in. He brought the calamity on himself.

Elihu believes that Job had said that the godly are no better off than the sinners, that Job is unrepentant and that he adds to his former sins by his rebellious words. Therefore Jobs deserves his suffering and will not get any relief from it. Job's suffering is because of his own wickedness.

The points that Elihu makes sounds right, but they are also dangerous. As he argues that God is right in everything that He does because He is sovereign, he makes the point that everything that happens is right. That does not, however, take into account the existence of evil. He also argues that every living thing depends on God for its being and that God may, at His discretion, take life away from His creatures. This is indeed a very good acknowledgement of God being the owner of everything in creation, but this argument leaves no room for any man to testify and say that God did something good. These arguments bring Elihu rather close to the points that Job made. However, Elihu falls back on a doctrine of 'might makes right' and that God rewards each person based on their deeds.

Elihu also argues, again, that Job deserved to be where he was at. Elihu was very harsh in his judgements and arguments. It was Job's own sins that brought him to where he was. His subsequent arguments made him doubly guilty. We know this is not true. This is clear from the first two chapters of the book.

The picture that Elihu presented here is that of a very harsh God. That is not true. God is a Father. He is a parent. Some of you are parents. There were times in the lives of your young children when they were disobedient. You might have said something like "Don't play in the streets." As a punishment, you would never have thought of letting your children lie down in front of your car and driving over their arms to teach them a lesson. If you as a human being know not to do something like that, imagine how good God is to His children.

Lord, You are sovereign. You are also my Father. You are good. I cry out to You "Abba Father." In Jesus; Name I pray. Amen.

God Rejoices Over His Children

"The Lord your God in your midst, the Mighty One will save; He will rejoice over you with gladness, He will quiet you with His love, He will rejoice over you with singing."

Zephaniah 3:17 (NKJV)

Zephaniah was a prophet. He was surrounded by sin. He knew of God's coming judgement on Israel and the surrounding nations. However, he also knew that God is merciful, ready, willing, able, and eager to forgive.

We (human beings) are not perfect. We tend to mess up. That is okay. God does not want to punish us for the wrongs we do. In fact, He wants us to rely on Him. The crucifixion of Jesus restored us with God. His Blood has paid for our sin – all our mess and mistakes have been covered. When we have a heart surrendered to God, He rejoices over us.

The Hebrew word for 'rejoice' here means to dance, skip, leap and spin around in joy. Strong's Concordance defines it as "properly spin around (under the influence of any violent emotion). Yes, this is how God rejoices over His children when they surrender to Him.

Not only is God the Creator, but He is also the One who is in the midst of us, protecting us and defending us. We can always call on Him. We can always trust in Him. He does not change. He is able and willing, to save us. Through Jesus, He saved us from death. Through Jesus, He has given us an abundance of life.

There once was a young man who wanted to venture out into the world on his own. He asked his father for his inheritance and set off. At first, things went well. He lived a high life. He had money and partied every day. He made lots of new friends. However, his money ran out. His partying ways came to an end. All his friends deserted him. He could not even afford to eat and had to eat with the pigs. He fell on really hard times. In his desperation, he made a plan. He was going to return home and become a servant in his father's house. At least he would have something to eat. When he went home he found that his father was waiting for him. His father was standing outside, looking into the distance for him. As soon as the father saw him, he ran to him. That night the father prepared a feast to welcome him back. That father is our Father. He rejoices over us when we come to Him.

Lord, I surrender it all to You. Thank you for wildly rejoicing over me when I seek You. Thank you for being who You are, that You never change and that I can trust in You completely. In Jesus' Name I pray. Amen.

God Provides For His Work

"Let it be known to the king we went into the province of Judea, to the temple of the great God, which is being built with heavy stones, and timber is being laid in its walls; and this work goes on diligently and prospers in their hands."

Ezra 5: 8 (NKJV)

The Jews were given a king's command to rebuild the temple. However, they did not work on the project for about 16 years because of the opposition from their enemies. Both Hagai and Zechariah, prophets of Israel, began to stir up the people again.

This just shows that God never lets go of the calling He has on a person's life – even if that person had given up because of various obstacles.

The devil does not give up either. There will always be opposition to the work of God in one way or another. In this case, people from the surrounding area complained and some officials showed up. The devil, through these officials, tried to oppose the work of God from a legal perspective. The Jews were questioned about the authority and permission they had for rebuilding the temple.

Tatnai and Shethar-boznai were these officials. The Jews told them that Cyrus had decreed the temple to be rebuild. Both Tatnai and Shethar-boznai wanted an official excuse to stop the work. Therefore, they sent a report to king Darius to 'examine' the truth of the Jews' claim.

This was the same king Darius who loved Daniel. Daniel had spent many an afternoon witnessing to the king. God knew what was to come in the future and had already made a plan.

Not only were the Jews' claim found to be truthful, but king Darius had also guaranteed protection for the workers. He further gave the order to his provincial officials to provide the Jews with money and materials for the work of rebuilding the temple – in other words, the work was to be paid for by the government. Darius also made sure the Jews had enough animals and produce to re-establish the temple rituals.

Four years later, the temple was dedicated and the feasts of Passover and Unleavened Bread were celebrated.

For 30 years, Lindsay Hamon has been carrying his life-sized cross across Europe and Asia as a way of starting conversations with people – conversations that opens the door for him to share the gospel. Right from the start, God provided for him. He had to go to bible school. An opportunity arose. He worked on a farm, picking fruit. He managed to save 1 000 Swiss Francs. The farmer then gave him another 1 000 Swiss Francs to pay for his studies. Back in 1980 he had printed the gospel in a booklet. It cost £40, which was quite a lot of money at the time. He got a tax rebate of £40 the next day. Once in New Zealand a stranger gave him £50. In Romania, a deal fell through. He no longer had a place to stay. He met an American. The American gave him some money. Lindsay found a hotel. The room was exactly the amount the American had given him. Things like these has been happening to Lindsay ever since God had called him and gave him a vision.

God will provide for His work.

Lord, thank you that You know the future. Thank you that there is nothing that catches You by surprise. Thank you that You always provide for Your work. Amen.

Labour To Rest

"Let us labour therefore to enter into that rest, lest any man fall after the same example of disbelief."

Hebrews 4: 11 (NKJV)

This sounds like a contradiction. On the one hand, this verse talks about working while it also talks about resting. Does this mean that the Christian life is a hard-working life or is a passive one? The answer is simple: it is neither.

Years ago (1994 – 2001), I was at a missionary organization. After I had finished my training I joined another guy to work on a project. That project would have culminated in the writing of a book. However, after a year that guy resigned and the writing of the book became my responsibility. I had never written a book. My director also gave me a deadline for the book. To make matters worse, the type of information was not readily available. That book was the first of its kind at the time. Talk about being thrown into the deep end. I worked very hard on meeting my deadline. Sometimes I would even be in the office at 2 AM, just writing. Yes, I overdid it, but nobody can say that I didn't labour.

What about the resting part? A few years earlier a pastor said to me that God can hit a home run with a crooked bat. I knew that this was from God. I was confident that the book would be completed on time. My trust and faith was in God. The book was released literally minutes before the deadline. Today, more than 20 years later, I can see the impact that it's made.

That is what it means to "labour to enter rest." We work, but at the same time, we trust in God. While we work, we also rest.

Father, thank you for letting us rest while we work. Thank you for the guidance of Your Spirit. Thank you for providing everything, including rest, we need when following Your Spirit. Amen.

Meditating On God's Word

"This book of the Law shall not depart from your mouth, but you shall meditate in it day and night, that you may observe to do according to all that is written in it. For then you will make your way prosperous, and then you will have good success."

Joshua 1:8 (NKJV)

Joshua was a godly man. He knew God's Word was true and to be acted upon. He knew that to meditate on it was wise and to neglect it would be a recipe for disaster. Just like Joshua did, we need to constantly think about God's word, ponder it in our hearts and act on it. This is the key to success. An important note: success is not measured in material possessions, but is based on eternal spiritual wealth.

It is important to know the Word of God. It is of critical importance to trust it. It is essential to apply it to our daily lives and to act on it. Circumstances does not matter, for everything works out for the good for those who trust the Lord (Romans 8: 28). By constantly thinking on God's Word, memorizing Scriptures, we meditate on it and feed our spirits. By trusting God instead of looking at reality and circumstances, we can expect things to work out for our good.

The bible could not be any clearer: the key to a successful and prosperous life is to meditate on God's Word and to act on it.

A woman in South Africa was afraid to drive. She was even afraid to go to sleep at night. She began meditating on God's Word. She memorized Scriptures and spoke them out whenever she felt anxious. As a result her one-year-old business is thriving, she is no longer afraid to drive and she can now enjoy a peaceful night's rest – even with the bedroom's door wide open!

Father, thank you for Your Word. Thank you for giving me the Scriptures. Holy Spirit, I ask that You'd help me to meditate on God's Word, to soak it up and to act on it. I pray this in the Name of Jesus, my Lord and Saviour. Amen.

Repentance Is Key

"Therefore because of you Zion shall be plowed like a field, Jerusalem shall become heaps of ruins, and the mountain of the temple like the bare hills of the forest."

Micah 3: 12 (NKJV)

The Israelites had a false sense of security. God had brought them out of Egypt, out of bondage, into the promised land. He had driven out the previous peoples. How can He ever allow the land to be captured by Israel's enemies? Jerusalem, the city of David, was where the sacred temple was, God's dwelling place amongst His people. How can this city and the temple ever be destroyed?

The nation's civil leaders became corrupt. Officials were greedy and worked hand in hand with corrupt judges to exploit people. Oppression was the order of the day. Sound familiar? The same thing is happening today in various countries across the world.

The religious leaders were corrupt too. Prophets only prophesied good things to those who were good to them. Negative prophesy was reserved for those who refused to be part of the corruption. The priests did various religious ceremonies only for those who paid them well.

Over a century later, Jeremiah quoted Micah in his own prophecy. Obviously the judgment and destruction that Micah prophesied did not happen. What happened? King Hezekiah heard Micah's prophecy. He acted on it, repented and turned back to God. That act of repentance turned away God's judgment. Even today we need to repent, turn to God and know that only He is our shield, our defence and our Saviour. Jeremiah quoted Micah, appealing to his own tormentors for leniency. During Jeremiah's time the people did not repent and destruction came.

There was a prophet who had to go to a city and prophecy doom over them. He prophesied the destruction of their city. People repented, 40 000 of its citizens heard the message and turned to God. As a result, the city was spared. That city was Nineveh. The prophet was Jonah.

Repentance is a key aspect of Christianity.

Holy Spirit I ask You to help me to always be just, to act in righteousness and to make sure that justice is done. I never want to be corrupt in any way. I declare my dependence on You oh Lord. In Jesus' Name I pray. Amen.

Be Humble, Repent And Seek God

"Then the Lord appeared to Solomon by night, and said to him: 'I have heard your prayer, and have chosen this place for Myself as a house of sacrifice. When I shut up heaven and there is no rain, or command the locusts to devour the land, or send pestilence among My people, if My people who are called by My Name will humble themselves, and pray and seek my face, and turn from their wicked ways, then I will hear from heaven, and will forgive their sin and heal their land.'"

2 Chronicles 7: 12-14 (NKJV)

Solomon spent a number of years building the temple. In this chapter he dedicated it. There was a huge celebration. However, Solomon could also foresee the unfaithfulness of the Israelites. He prayed for them. After all the celebrations came to an end, God answered him.

God told Solomon that when Israel turned away from Him there would be consequences. However, He also said that if they were to come back to Him that He will restore them. This shows God's willingness to reverse judgment when people repent.

This is very true of the world we live in today. All over the world, people have moved away from God. We desperately need God – in our personal lives, in our communities and in our nations across the world. When we turn to God, He will forgive, heal and restore. It is His promise. We need to humble ourselves and seek God.

God went on to warn Solomon not to forsake Him. Often times God also warns us. As many times as God warns us, we tend to think that those warnings are not applicable to us. Solomon ended up forsaking the Lord – the very thing God warned him against. It is tragic. We need to heed God's warnings.

After World War II, a holocaust survivor returned to Germany to declare forgiveness through Jesus. After her sermon, a man came to her to ask forgiveness. She recognised him. He was one of the most cruel guards at the Nazi concentration camp she was imprisoned at. It is also the same camp where her sister had died. All sorts of emotions went through her. She realized though that to forgive was an act of the will and that God had forgiven her own sins over and over again. Finally she managed to speak the words "I forgive you." This is what she wrote about that encounter. "I stood there – I whose sins had again and again been forgiven – and could not forgive. It could have been many seconds that he stood there – hand held out – but to me it seemed like hours as I wrestled with the most difficult thing I ever had to do. I had to do it – I knew that. The message that God forgives has a prior condition: that we forgive those who have injured us. I prayed silently 'Jesus help me'" She then goes on. "The current started in my shoulder, raced down my arm, and sprang into our joined hands. And then this healing warmth seemed to flood my whole being, bringing tears to my eyes. 'I forgive you, brother!' I cried.'With all my heart.'. I had never known love so intensely as I did then. Even then, I realized it was not my love, but the power of the Holy Spirit." That woman was Corrie Ten Boom.

God is extremely responsive when we repent and seek Him.

Lord, I always want to follow You. I do not want to forsake You. Help me, Holy Spirit, to testify like the Psalmist and say that Your Word is a lamp unto my feet. In Jesus Name I pray. Amen.

Selah

"All Scripture is is given by inspiration of God, and is profitable for doctrine, for reproof, for correction, for instruction in holiness, that the man of God may be complete, thoroughly equipped for every good work."

2 Timothy 3:16-17 (NKJV)

In a number of Psalms, we see the word "selah." If Scripture was given to us through the Holy Spirit, then there is a reason why that word is there. The Holy Spirit wants to tell us something through that word. What does it mean and how do we apply it?

The Psalms are songs to God. "Selah" is a Hebrew musical instruction. It tells the musician to pause and have a break. That is what the Holy Spirit is telling us. He is saying that when the pressures of life overwhelm us, we need a break. We need to stop and reflect on God's character, His goodness, and what He has done for us in the past. This will lead to us being rejuvenated. We'll be able to keep on moving forward.

Years ago, in South Africa, there was a KitKat ad. It said, "Have a break, have a KitKat." That is what the Holy Spirit is telling us. Stop, have a break and think about what God has done for you up until now.

Stop, have a break, have a selah.

Father, thank you for Your goodness, Your mercy and Your grace. Thank you for not leaving me to my own devices. Holy Spirit I ask that You will always bring to my remembrance the things that Jesus did, what He has done for me personally. Amen.

Trust: A Principle Of Faith

"And he believed in the Lord, and He accounted it to him for righteousness."

Genesis 15:6 (NKJV)

At a very old age God told Abraham that he was going to have a son. In the natural, it is impossible to father any children at that advanced age. However, he decided to believe God. God put in his account righteousness.

I once heard a story of a man that went to climb a mountain. Halfway up he realised that he was not going to reach the summit before nightfall. Instead of looking for shelter and then continuing the next day, the man decided to push ahead. It became very dark, bitterly cold and he was disorientated. He missed his grip and fell. Eventually, his safety equipment kicked in. The rope that was attached to his harness arrested his fall. While hanging there, he called out to God and asked Him to save him. God told him to cut his rope. This made him afraid. The next day, a search-and-rescue team found a man, frozen to death, hanging from a rope. The man was still clutching the rope. He was 3ft. from the ground.

One man believed God. It was accounted to him as righteousness. Another man trusted his own judgement and died.

Lord Jesus thank you for Your Blood and crucifixion. You have made me righteous. You have put me in a right standing with God. In Your Name I pray, Lord Jesus. Amen.

The Armour Of God

"Therefore take up the whole armour of God that you may be able to withstand in the evil day, and having done all, to stand. Stand therefore, having girded your waist with truth, having put on the breastplate of righteousness, and having shod your feet with the preparation of the gospel of peace; above all, taking the shield of faith with which you will be able to quench all the fiery darts of the wicked one. And take the helmet of salvation, and the sword of the Spirit, which is the word of God."

Ephesians 6: 13-17 (NKJV)

Life can be very hard. Things go wrong and people turn against you. What to do?

It is important to keep in mind that everything is spiritual. The bible says in Ephesians 6:12 that we do not wrestle against flesh and blood, but against principalities, powers and rulers of dark places. Our struggle is against the forces of darkness. Even though it will be emotionally gratifying to lash out against flesh and blood, it will not resolve anything. God has given us armour.

The first apparel of the armour is the belt of truth (Eph. 6:14). What does this mean and how do we apply it? A belt keeps pants in place. It prevents the wearer to be exposed. The truth here does not only refer to us not telling lies, but to the whole truth of who Jesus is and what He has done. Knowing who Jesus is and what He has done will prevent us from following the wrong doctrine. The truth is that we are free – irrespective of what we do. God has punished sin. Through Jesus we have liberty. Our freedom and salvation are not based on our behaviour, but on what God has done, it is based on His grace. That is what gives us identity, what holds everything in place.

The second piece of the armour is the breastplate of righteousness (Eph. 6:14). Think of Roman soldiers at that time. A breastplate is worn as protection for the chest. Inside of the chest is the heart. The heart symbolises the spirit. Jesus has made us righteous. In a nutshell: we are in right standing with God.

The next article is the sandals on the feet (Eph. 6:15). Wearing shoes protects the feet against thorns and all sorts of elements. It enables the wearer to be able to move when required to do so. Being ready to share the gospel with others has the same effect in the spiritual realm. Because of what Jesus did, we can experience peace in spite of our circumstances. This is what the gospel gives us. We have the peace of God that surpasses all understanding. It is this peace that allows us to stand.

The shield of faith is extremely important (Eph. 6:16). Having complete faith in God enables us to withstand the attacks from the devil. This means knowing who God is. It is not a question of "Will He do it for me?" It is a matter of knowing that God will do things because He said a number of things in His Word. It is knowing that God is faithful even when we are not (2 Tim. 2:13), He is true to His Word (Numbers 23:19) and He is able to perform it (Jer. 1:12 and Is. 55:6-11).

Next we have the helmet of salvation. A helmet is worn on the head (obviously). It protects the brain. Our souls are basically in our brains. This is where we have intellect, will and emotions. Salvation protects our souls. What is salvation? Jesus is the Way, the Truth and the Life (John 14:6). He has made us victorious (1 Cor. 15:57). He has healed us (1 Peter 2:24). He has given us life (John 10:10). These are just a few of the benefits of salvation. We need to think about these constantly and meditate on them.

The last part of the armour is the sword of the Spirit, which is the Word of God (Eph. 6:17). A sword can be used for both defense and offense. Knowing what the Word says enables us to know the truth and to deliver knock-out punches to lies.

To wrap things up we can say that even though we face physical challenges, they can be overcome by using the armour that God gave us. Even though challenges are physical, they need to be fought in the spiritual realm. That is the only way to effectively and successfully deal them.

Lord, thank you for having gave me armour to live victoriously. Holy Spirit, help me to use the armour, and to use them correctly. In Jesus' Name I pray. Amen.

An Unshakable Foundation

"For since by man came death, by Man also came the resurrection of the dead. For as in Adam all die, even so in Christ all shall be made alive."

1 Corinthians 15: 21-22 (NKJV)

Jesus died for our sins and was resurrected again. He is alive; because of this we are forgiven and have been made alive. The resurrection of Jesus is living proof of this fact.

The bible tells us that our sins have been removed "as far as the east is from the west." The earth has a north pole and a south pole. There is a point where one can't go any further north or south. However, no matter we are on earth, we can always go further east or west.

Being forgiven is not based on what we did or did not do. It is based on God's goodness, His grace. Jesus' finished work at the cross enables us to receive the gift of salvation. A gift is not something one works for, earns or deserves. It is given. Jesus gave His own life as a ransom for ours.

We deserved punishment for our sins. We deserved death. However, Jesus took that death, paid the price for all our sin (past, present and future) and gave us eternal life. We are saved by grace through faith. It is His unmerited, unearned and undeserved favour.

We are saved. We are forgiven. We have been made righteous. Righteousness is not about doing right, but about believing what the right thing is. When we accept Jesus as Lord and Saviour, we become righteous. This is how God sees us. This is our unshakable foundation. We can build on this foundation. Never allow any teaching that makes you work for these things. Jesus did it. It is finished. Amen.

Jesus told the story of a man who built his house on the sand, while another was built on the rocks. When the storm came, the house with its foundation on the sand fell, while the other remained standing. In the same way, Jesus is our foundation. In life we will face difficulties, but because of Jesus we can remain standing. He is our foundation. No storm can move Him.

Lord Jesus, You are my foundation. You are bigger than my circumstances. Because of You, I can face tomorrow. In Your Name I pray. Amen.

Finding Your Purpose

"...All things were created through Him and for Him."

Colossians 1: 16

We have been created for God. We are His. We are not our own, but belong to Him. Jesus bought us at a price. Ask yourself the following questions: Is what I do bringing glory to God? Does my work/career/job drain me or energise me? Do I peace and joy in what I do?

Jesus said that all those who are heavy burdened should go to Him for His yoke is light. Doing what God has created you to do will result in you having a positive impact on people around you. I have lost nine years of my life doing the wrong thing. Do not settle for anything less than what God has created you for.

Often times, we looked at the economy to determine our future. We studied a field that was in demand. If that field was not something that God created you for, you would have found that job to be draining, maybe even affording you less time with your family and even less time with God.

We have been called for two things. Our first calling is to be in fellowship with the Son, to have a relationship with Jesus (1 John 1: 3). The second calling is specific, our jobs: doctors, lawyers, teachers, farmers, etc. We have been bought at a price – we do not belong to ourselves. We should not live for selfish purposes or desires.

Michael (not his real name) grew up in a family where all his brothers and sisters were doctors. All of them were successful. He decided that he would become one as well. He studied into the medical field and became a doctor. He did not like it. He found it to be a strain not only on him, but also his family. To make matters worse, the hospital increased his shift, causing him to spend even less time with his family and with God. Eventually, he gave up and asked God what he should do. As it turned out, he was called into full-time ministry.

Lord Jesus, thank you for having bought me. Thank you for having called me into a relationship with God. Thank you for having a specific purpose for my life. In Your Name I pray, Lord Jesus. Amen.

A Righteous Advocate

*"Then he showed me Joshua the high priest standing before the Angel of the
Lord, and Satan standing at his right hand to oppose him."*

Zechariah 3: 1 (NKJV)

Joshua was the high priest of Israel during Zechariah's time. In this
vision, he was not physically in the presence of God, but ministering,
doing his priestly duties and representing the religious aspects of the
nation of Israel. Satan was standing at his right, opposing him.

That is so in Satan's character. He hates it when people come to God,
when people enter into His presence, honouring and serving Him. In
this vision, the bible also tells us that Joshua was clothed in filthy
garments. Satan must have pointed to those, accusing Joshua, saying that
Joshua was not fit for office. The name Satan literally means 'adversary'
or 'opponent.'

He still does that today, pointing to people's faults. When the children of
God sin, the devil sees it. He then accuses them, trying to get them to be
sentenced. He tries to make people feel like they are not worthy to be of
any use to God.

However, the children of God have Someone who stands up for them. In the vision, the Angel of the Lord was also present. He was standing in front of Satan, preventing his advance. That Angel is Jesus. Even though God does allow Satan to attack His people, Satan is strictly regulated. When Satan accuses the saints of God, Jesus defends them.

Joshua, the high priest was dressed in filthy garments, but it got changed. The same with us. Jesus is our righteousness. He is our Prince and High Priest. We have been pardoned! Because of this, we can have peace.

Jesus warned one of his disciples, Simon Peter, of Satan's plans. Satan wanted to destroy him, to 'sift' him like weed. However, Jesus prayed for Peter. He stood beside him and defended him. Satan's plan was opposed. Jesus stood in his way. Because of Jesus, Satan could not carry out the evil in his heart.

Lord Jesus, thank you for defending me. Thank you for being my advocate. Thank you for having pardoned me. In Your Name I pray, Lord Jesus. Amen.

Our Escape

"But you, brethren, are not in darkness, so that this Day should overtake you as a thief."

1 Thessalonians 5: 4 (NKJV)

The Thessalonian Christians suffered great persecution. Their persecution was so great that they thought it was the day of Lord as prophesied before by the prophet Joel. It is against this backdrop that Paul writes to them.

The day of the Lord, as described by Joel, is a terrible time. It is a time of darkness for unbelievers. It is a time when God's judgement and wrath comes upon the earth. For too long have men turned away from God and followed their own 'wisdom.' I remember, as a child, things like homosexuality, divorce, pre-marital sex, teenage pregnancies, abortions and the like were considered to be social evils. Today, these things have become the norm, and is even expected in some cases. It is important to not reject the people caught up in these, but we must condemn the lifestyles and choices. The day of Lord here is also known as the tribulation.

There are only two types of people in the world: the believer and the unbeliever, the saved and the damned. The saved are the Christians – the true followers of Jesus. They belong to the light. The unbeliever belong to darkness. This day of the Lord is described as being very dark indeed.

Fortunately, the believer won't experience the day of the Lord. Paul is describing an event known as the rapture to the Thessalonians. In this present age, Christians will face persecution, but not the wrath of God. Jesus will remove His people from the earth.

Just as solders must always be prepared for battle, so too must the believer be prepared for Christ's return. That means that they must live self-controlled lives, be strong in faith and love and be confident in their salvation. The believer must have a relationship with God and be in fellowship with other brethren.

Recently, I heard a prophecy about the rapture. The scene described people being on holiday. They were in boats on the river. Some were swimming while others were sunbathing. All of a sudden, the people started murmuring. They saw flashes in the sky and started to point at these flashes. Multitudes of angels came down, moving at the speed of light. They removed God's people. Others were left behind and faced the wrath of God.

My plea is that you would make right with God. Accept Jesus as your Lord and Saviour while you still can.

Lord Jesus, thank you for having redeemed me. Thank you, Holy Spirit, for sealing me as belonging to Jesus. I ask that many more people will be saved. In Jesus' Name I pray. Amen.

Talking With God

"Continue earnestly in prayer, being vigilant in it with thanksgiving;"

Colossians 4: 2 (NKJV)

God wants a relationship with us. It is not because He is lonely – He has existed even before the foundation the earth. Neither is it because we are special. He wants a relationship with us because He chose to love us.

Prayer should not be limited to an event, something to be done only on special occasions. It is meant to be an ongoing dialogue with the Lord.

Paul tells the Colossians to pray with thanksgiving. Jesus bought us with His blood. Through His crucifixion, He has put us in a right standing with God, He has redeemed us. That is reason enough to be thankful. Because of this, there is nothing stopping us from being in a relationship with God. Prayer is basically the vehicle through which we talk to God. Furthermore, through prayer God imparts to us.

No one is more praise-worthy than God. There are plenty of reasons to praise Him and to worship Him. Prayer is the vehicle through which we offer thanks, praise and worship to God.

God assures us that He hears our prayers. What an amazing thought, what an awesome privilege. The Creator of the entire universe listens to us, He hears our prayers and cries. We have the freedom to go to Him with all our requests. Our prayers should not be emotionless. We are encouraged to pour our hearts out to Him.

Somebody once asked C. S. Lewis why, if God knows everything and is sovereign, they should pray. He answered: "You might as well ask me 'why breathe,' for prayer to the soul is as necessary as breathing is to the body." A study found that people who prayed had normal levels of cortisol and stresses less often. Praying is good for an individual's health. The practice is recommended by experts.

Lord Jesus, thank you for having put me in a right standing with God. Lord Jesus, You have made it possible for me to talk with the Creator of the universe. Thank you Father, for hearing my prayers. In Jesus' Name I pray. Amen.

The Responsibility Of A Sentinel

"Again the word of the Lord came to me, saying, Son of man, speak to the children of your people, and say to them: 'When I bring the sword upon a land and the people of the land take a man from their territory and make him their watchman, when he sees the sword coming upon the land, if he blows the trumpet and warns the people, then whoever hears the sound of the trumpet and does not take warning, if the sword comes and takes him away, his blood shall be on his own head."

Ezekiel 33: 1-4 (NKJV)

Ezekiel was held personally responsible to proclaim God's judgement, just like a watchman or sentinel is responsible for sounding the alarm bell. In order to relieve himself of the responsibility, he had to tell the people to repent.

Just as Ezekiel was held personally responsible, we as Christians are also responsible to call others to live justly, to repent and turn to God. In the Old Testament only a few people were called to be prophets, proclaimers of God's Word. However, under the New Covenant all Christians have a responsibility. After all, the prophet Joel did prophesy that God will pour out His Spirit on all flesh in the end times. We are to be sentinels.

In the workplace for example, Christians should for justice, showing no partiality and speaking God's words. We are not to let pressure get to us so that we can fit in. Being a sentinel is not being judgemental, but it does mean that we are supposed to stand up for the truth, even if that stance is an unpopular one.

We are also to live lives worthy of our calling, honouring God. Ezekiel was a visual and walking illustration of God's promises and judgements.

Ben (not his real name) is a New Zealander. He likes to stay fit and exercises regularly. He went swimming in the ocean one day and saw a dolphin swimming close to him. Ben had his camcorder with him and recorded the scene. When he got home, he looked at the footage. That is when he saw it. A shark was stalking him. However, the shark never came close because the dolphin was there. The dolphin kept watch.

Lord, You have called me into Your marvelous light. You saved me. Help me, Holy Spirit, to step out in boldness and proclaim Your word, to live a life that glorifies and honours You and not to turn a blind eye to the truth. In Jesus' Name I pray. Amen.

God Is In Control

"Now when Herod was dead, behold, an angel of the Lord appeared in a dream to Joseph in Egypt saying, 'Arise, take the young Child and His mother, and go to the land of Israel, for those who sought the young Child's life are dead.' Then He arose, took the young Child and His mother, and came to the land of Israel. But when he heard that Archelaus was reigning over Judea instead of his father Herod, he was afraid to go there. And being warned by God in a dream, he turned aside into the region of Galilee. He came and dwelt in a city called Nazareth, that it might be fulfilled which was spoken by the prophets, 'He shall be called a Nazarene.'

Matthew 2: 19-23 (NKJV)

Herod felt threatened. He issued a command. It was a command that saw babies being massacred. Joseph took his wife and their Child, Jesus, and fled to Egypt.

Both Israel and Egypt were provinces of the Roman Empire. Herod was the governor of Judea. His influence, reach and jurisdiction did not extend to Egypt. He was now dead and therefore Joseph could return to Israel. However, Joseph became afraid when he learned that Archelaus, the son of Herod, was now the governor. God guided him into another region.

Jesus grew up and taught the people. He was known as the Man from Galilee, the Nazarene. He fulfilled His earthly ministry. He became our Lord and Saviour. He brought salvation to the Human race. Even though Satan tried to stop the Son of God, God always was in control. He always knew what to do.

As we surrender to Him, He still works out things for His glory. It may not always be in the way we thought, but He is still in control.

In 1982, a pastor's wife suffered from a stroke. The pastor was devastated. He loved his wife more than his own life. In the hospital, the doctor told him that his wife would be moved to another unit for rehabilitation, that there wasn't anything they could do for her any more. He told his wife about the development and added that God was in control. Even though he did not understand why these things were happening, he knew that God is sovereign. As the years went by, he learned from David's example in the Psalms about the sovereignty of God. Now we only know in part, but one day we will be able to see the big picture. The stroke his wife suffered already lead to him searching the Scriptures, realising certain truths and learning about the sovereignty of God. Even the stroke his wife suffered was used by God for His glory. It is not that God had planned the stroke or deliberately inflicted this on his wife, but even through that He is still sovereign and uses the negative circumstances to bring glory to His Name.

Lord, You are always in control. You are sovereign. Even though I may not understand why things are happening, my trust is in You. You know. Everything is for Your glory. In Jesus' Name I pray. Amen.

Growing Through Trials

"When I heard, my body trembled; my lips quivered at the voice; rottenness entered my bones; ans I trembled in myself, that I might rest in the day of trouble. When he comes up to the people, he will invade them with his troops. Though the fig tree may not blossom, nor fruit be on the vines; though the labour of the olive may fail, and the fields yield no food; though the flock may be cut off from the fold and there be no herd in the stalls – yet I will rejoice in the Lord, I will joy in the God of my salvation. The Lord God is my strength; He will make my feet like deer's feet, and He will make me walk on my high hills."

Habakkuk 3: 16-19 (NKJV)

Habakkuk heard some very frightening news. The news was terrible. His people and his country was going into a period of intense trials. Things were going to get worse before they got better. Habakkuk experienced a number of different emotions, including fear. He was overwhelmed.

We also experience emotions. That is not wrong. It is what we allow that will determine the outcome. In a case like this, we have two options. Either we can let our emotions take a hold us and be lead by them, or we can decide to wait patiently to see what God is going to do. Habakkuk felt distraught, but he took his emotions to God. He decided to trust God and rest in Him. We should never allow worry to get the better of us, but we should always look to God, trust Him and know, that in spite of everything around us, He is still good.

The Israelites were an agriculture based society. Habakkuk uses imagery that they could understand to describe his resolve. All the produce used here are long-term investments, they take up to five years to bear fruit. Farmers, having put in a lot hard work before hand, depended on these crops for their livelihoods. Habakkuk says that even if he did not see the fruit of his labour, he will still trust and rejoice in the Lord. We need to make the same decision. Instead of trials wearing us down, we should look to Jesus. We should know and trust that God is still on the throne.

In his prophesy, Habakkuk said that the Israelites were going to face defeat and exile. It would take hundreds of years for them to return. Even though this is a tough reality to face, it is the very thing that God used to turn their hearts back to them. Trials in our own lives builds character. Joy does not depend on our circumstances.

The end result of the decision to turn to the Lord? Strength. Habakkuk ends off with him saying that the Lord is his strength, that the Lord will make his footsteps secure. Having endured the trial and turned to God, He will enable you to conquer.

Exercising the body makes the muscles stronger. Pain and suffering are needed for the body to develop. Even little children stumble and fall, preparing them to walk better. Growing up involves getting hurt through bumps and bruises. However, these bumps and bruises prepares the child for a physical life. In the same way, trials strengthen the soul and grows the faith.

Lord, You are always in control – even in the trials I face. Holy Spirit, help me to realise that everything works together for my benefit because I trust in You. In Jesus' Name I pray. Amen.

God Is Love

"He who does not love does not know God, for God is love."

1 John 4: 8

To know God requires of us to have a relationship with Him. Love is a characteristic of God. Love is an integral part of a Christian's life, because it is part of God's identity.

God showed His love for people through Jesus. Jesus, the Son of God, came to earth, ministered to people on earth and died for our sins. He paid the price for our redemption.

God loved us first, when we were still sinners. It is through Him that we can show others the love of God. We can demonstrate His love to the world because we have become His children, He enables us to do so. The love of God can not be humanly reproduced. People may be able to demonstrate human affection, but divine love is a spiritual fruit, manifested in the life of person who has a relationship with the one true God.

Just like God demonstrated His love for us through Jesus, we too are supposed to demonstrate our love for one another. We are to think of others as more highly than ourselves. The needs of other believers should be considered before our own. Divine love is an action requiring of us to do what is best for our brethren. This brings honour to God.

Russell Herman died in 1994. In his will, he set aside $2 billion for East St. Louis, $2,5 for the department of forestry and $6 trillion for the government to pay off the national debt. Just one small problem. The only asset he had was a 1983 Oldsmobile. His words were empty. Jesus saw an old woman put in two mites in the Temple. She gave more than the will of the late Russell Herman. His were mere wishes, hers was given from the heart. She showed her love for God.

Father, thank you for loving me so much that You gave Your only begotten Son as a sacrifice for me. Thank you for having loved me first. Holy Spirit, please help me to demonstrate Your love to others. In Jesus, Name I pray. Amen.

Useful Service

"But in a great house there are not only vessels of gold and silver, but also of wood and clay, some for honour and some for dishonour."

2 Timothy 2: 20

An analogy is used here. Firstly, there is the 'great house' and then also vessels made from different materials with different uses. The great house is the church of Jesus and the vessels are us, some were of more value than the earthen vessels used for everyday needs.

Like the valuable vessels of silver and gold not used for everyday activities, Timothy was to set himself apart for the ministry. He was to be used by God. He had to abstain from sin, he had to cleanse himself from 'dishonourable' uses.

God does use certain people for a certain purpose because He is sovereign. He is the potter and we are the clay. However, in this context, the extent to which we are useful to God is determined by our actions. Our usefulness is linked to our actions. We have a responsibility. There are several things we can do to become useful.

We must separate ourselves from ungodly relationships. Separate yourselves from worldly friends. Do not become entangled in their ways, no compromise, no love for any sin. As the Bible says, 'bad company corrupts good morals.' Test the teaching of others against the Word of God. Discern false teaching and false teachers from the truth. Be an approved follower of Christ, handling the truth correctly. We have a solid foundation in Jesus. We must flee all wickedness.

Before buying a car, one needs to look at several things. Does the car fulfill the needs it will be used for? Is the price tag within range? What sort of mileage can I expect from it? What reputation does the brand have?

When I was at World Mission Centre, our director, Willie Crew, used to say 'Your attitude will determine your altitude.'

Lord, thank you for wanting to use me for Your purpose. Holy Spirit, I ask that You will prepare me honourable service in the Master's Hands. In Jesus' Name I pray. Amen.

Praise God

"Therefore by Him let us continually offer the sacrifice of praise to God, that is, the fruit of our lips, giving thanks to His name."

Hebrews 13: 15 (NKJV)

Some Jews suffered persecution for their faith. The letter to the Hebrews were meant to encourage them.

It is easy to praise God when He has blessed us. However, praise is not an evaluation of His job performance and should never be treated as a reward for what He has done for us.

Jesus died on the cross. He was the perfect sacrifice. He took away our guilt and reconciled us with God. He made us righteous. He redeemed us. He paid the price. We have been forgiven. His work is complete and finished. There is nothing to be added.

During the hard times, we should still praise Him. When things don't work out as we think they should or God, in our opinions, does not come through like we expect Him to, we must still praise Him. It is then that praise becomes a sacrifice, the fruit of our lips. It is an act of the will. It is in praising God during these times that we show that we trust Him, in spite of circumstances screaming for us to do the opposite. He is always good and always trust-worthy.

Our praise should come from a place of joy. It is because of Jesus that we have hope, a living hope. He brought us salvation. He gave us life. Praise God always for He is good.

A young girl was diagnosed with a debilitating throat disease. She could not sing any more. She attended a faith conference and decided to sing unto God for the victory that Jesus gained. In that meeting, God healed her. She described it as her throat that had popped open. Despite of the debilitating diagnoses, she chose to worship God. She did not allow bad news to dictate to her, but chose to praise God, trusting in His good nature.

Father, thank you for the sacrifice of Your Son. Thank you that I am forgiven. Lord, You are always good. You are praise-worthy. You are trust-worthy. You are good. Help me, Holy Spirit, to never lose sight of that. In Jesus' Name I pray. Amen.

Also by Morne Campher

Wisdom For Everyday
The Spirit Filled Life
Food For Thought

About the Author

Morne Campher was a missionary for seven years. He has a passion for the lost and a desire to see every believer walk in a closer and more intimate relationship with God.

9 7 9 8 2 1 5 3 5 3 4 7 9